勞工節

Customs, Traditions and Landmarks |
Non-Fiction Series

Copyright © 2022 by Level Learning, INC. and Washington Yu Ying PCS™
Original and Edited Text Copyright © 2022 by Washington Yu Ying PCS™

All rights reserved. No part of this book in whole or part may be reproduced without written permission from the publisher.

Published by Level Learning

Content Contributors:
Washington Yu Ying PCS™
Level Learning - Ya-Ching Chang

Illustrations by: Josh Taira

Leveling classification based on Level Learning standard. For full description, visit www.levellearning.com

ISBN 978-1-64040-029-0
Traditional Chinese Edition

About Level Learning:
Level Learning provides a literacy focused curriculum specifically designed for K-12 Chinese as a Second Language classrooms. Our program offers 20 levels of specific and detailed objectives, leveled texts and passages, mastery-based online assessment, and analytics to enable data-driven instruction. Level Learning reading curriculum for both literature and informational text emphasize grammar and comprehension skills to help teachers develop confident and independent Chinese language readers. The non-fiction series of books are specifically designed to support our informational text course based on multiple national standards. To learn more about our entire offering, visit www.levellearning.com.

About Washington Yu Ying PCS™:
Washington Yu Ying PCS is a Mandarin English dual language immersion International Baccalaureate (IB) World school. Yu Ying's mission is to inspire and prepare young people to create a better world by challenging them to reach their full potential in a nurturing Chinese/English educational environment. Yu Ying's comprehensive IB, dual immersion curriculum equips students with global competencies for success in the real world. As a leader in immersion education, Yu Ying is determined to advance Chinese language programs and global citizenry education by helping other schools create and strengthen their Chinese programs. For more information, email: products@washingtonyuying.org

九月

星期一	星期二	星期三	星期四	星期五	星期六	星期日
	1	2	3	4	5	6
7	8	9	10	11	12	13
14	15	16	17	18	19	20
21	22	23	24	25	26	27
28	29	30				

每年九月的第一個星期一，是美國的勞工節。

在勞工節假期，很多人不用去工作，學生們也不用去上學。

為什麼美國有勞工節假期呢?

1882年9月5日,紐約市有一群工人上街遊行。這群工人希望有更多的休息時間。他們也希望得到更多收入。

那時候的工人，工作時間很長，收入卻很少。

後來，每年九月的第一個星期，紐約市的工人都會上街遊行。其他地方的工人知道了，也都上街遊行。他們的希望被大家聽到了。

在1894年,美國把每年九月的第一個星期一定為勞工節。多年以後,工人一星期只要工作四十個小時。因此,工人們有了更多的時間休息,也得到了更多的收入。

有了勞工節假期，大家也有時間做不同的活動。有些人會去旅行，有些人會看球賽。

你的勞工節假期會做什麼呢?

Glossary

	Pinyin	English Definition
勞工節	láo gōng jié	Labor Day
假期	jià qī	holiday
紐約市	niǔ yuē shì	New York City
一群	yì qún	a group
上街遊行	shàng jiē yóu xíng	street parade
希望	xī wàng	to hope
更多	gèng duō	more
收入	shōu rù	income
卻	què	but
其他	qí tā	other
聽到	tīng dào	to hear
定為	dìng wéi	set, establish
小時	xiǎo shí	hours
旅行	lǚ xíng	vacation
看	kàn	to watch

	Pinyin	English Definition
球賽	qiú sài	sporting events